BIBLE POP.com™

Presents

OFFICER DO-GOOD and His Friends

Coloring Book

written by **Dominic Francese**   illustrated by **Nick Nix**

BIBLE POP.com

Copyright © 2012 Biblepop.com, LLC
Published by Biblepop.com, LLC
P.O. Box 383
Carmel, IN 46082 USA
ISBN: 0615631428
ISBN-13: 978-0615631424

CONTENTS

Crazy Columbus

Christopher Columbus
read the Bible, and he
believed God chose him to
bring the words of Jesus
to those who had
never heard them.

He also believed the world
was round even though most
people at that time
did not agree.

He believed that by sailing
west he could find a shortcut
to China. Then he would
have gold and jewels,
and be very rich!

He explained his ideas to
the queen of Spain, and she
agreed to pay for the voyage to
the West.

Columbus set off with his
three ships and his men.
They had enough provisions
for a year of sailing.

But his men became
very scared.

After all, everyone knew
the world was flat!

They thought that they were
going to fall off the edge!

They wanted Columbus to
turn around and head home.

There was talk of mutiny.

Now, Columbus was a religious
man and believed God's
Holy Spirit was with him.

He got down on his knees
and began to pray,
"My God, please help me!

"My men think they will
never see any land again, and
now they want to throw me
overboard and take over
the ship!"

Then one day, far
away, they saw land!
God had answered
Columbus's prayer!

"Aha, you see?
I told you so,"
Columbus said.

Columbus became very
famous because he had
discovered the New World.

Columbus didn't find
gold and riches,
and he didn't find a
shortcut to China.

But he accomplished something
even more important: He brought
the words of Jesus across the
seas, just as he believed
God chose him to do.

To this day, many
people in the New World
still believe the
words of Jesus . . .

. . . all because of
Christopher Columbus!

My dog Nina!

My Dog Nina!

We've got a dog at our house.
My wife and kids just love her.
Her name is Nina.

She thinks my girls are her sisters.
She thinks my wife is her mother.

But as for me, she stares at me
with a naughty, doggie grin.

And then she looks around the room
for some trouble to get in.

One time I was making a sandwich, and then I got to thinking.

I noticed out of my window
that my sprinklers hadn't
stopped sprinkling.

So I went outside to turn them off,
and I stepped in from the lawn.

But when I got back to my plate,
my sandwich—it was gone!

I saw her down the hallway.
It was hanging from her mouth.

So I chased her up and
down the stairs and around
and around the house.

I cornered her and grabbed it
with a tug and a pull and a push.

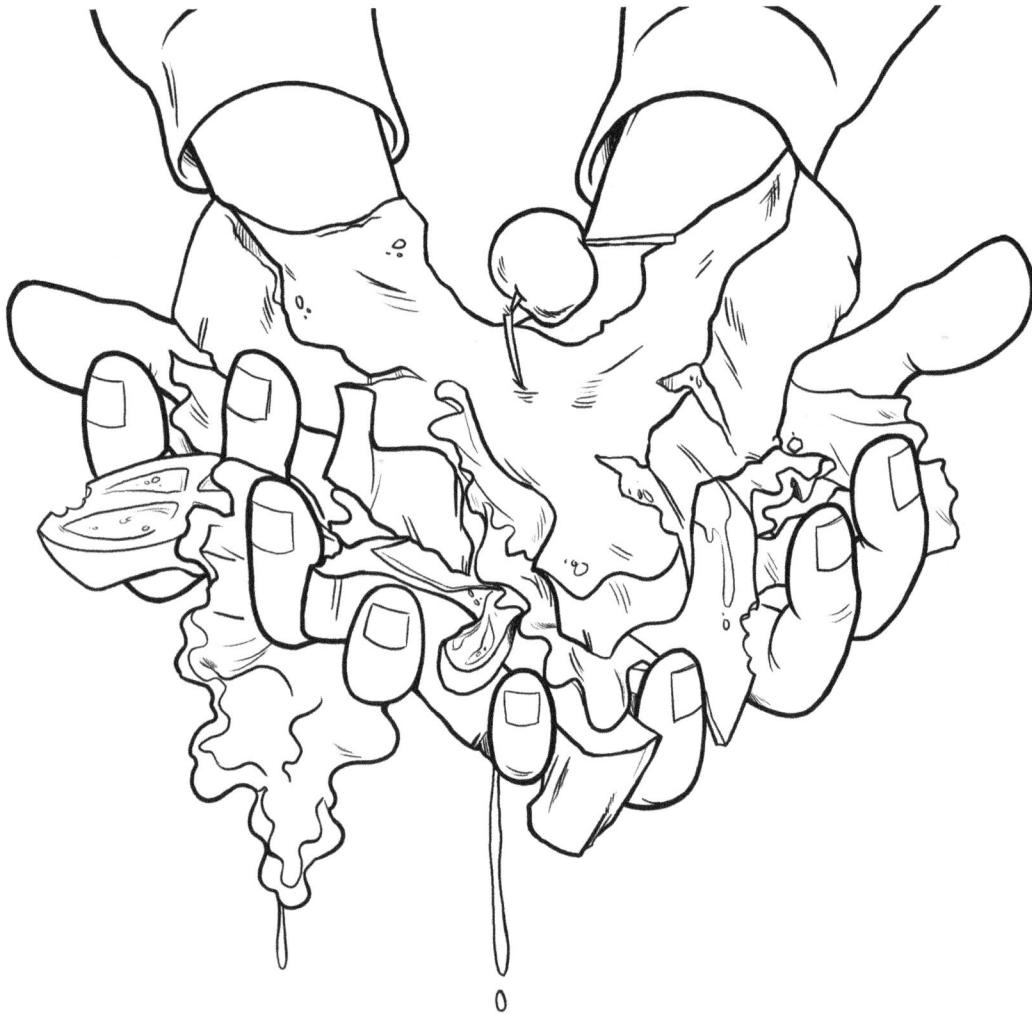

But all that I could rescue
was a bunch of doggie mush.

One time I took a shower.
I got clean underwear.

I placed it next to the bathroom sink thinking it would be right there.

I showered and I dried off,
and went to put it on.

But when I reached for my
underwear, my underwear
was . . . gone!

I saw her down the hallway.
It was hanging from her mouth.

So I chased her up and down
the stairs and around and
around the house.

I cornered her and grabbed it,
and we started a tug of war.

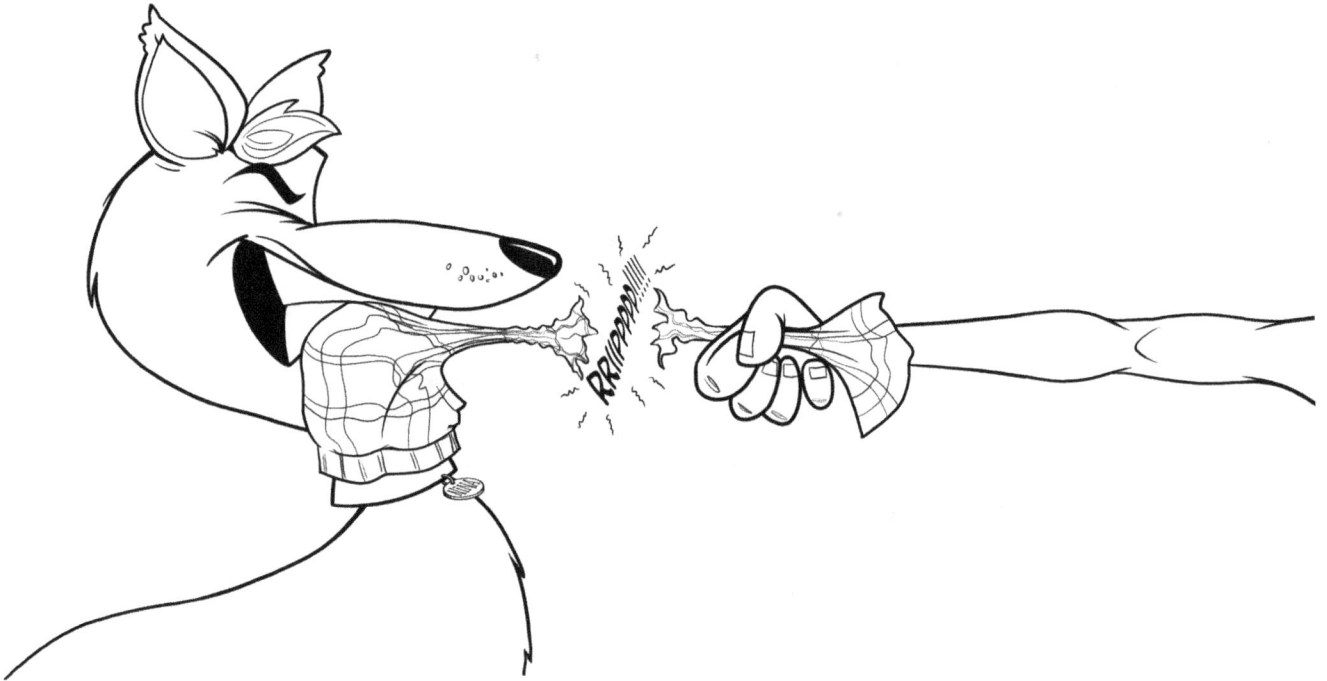

We pushed and pulled it
back and forth till finally
it tore!

Then I heard my youngest girl
calling from behind me.

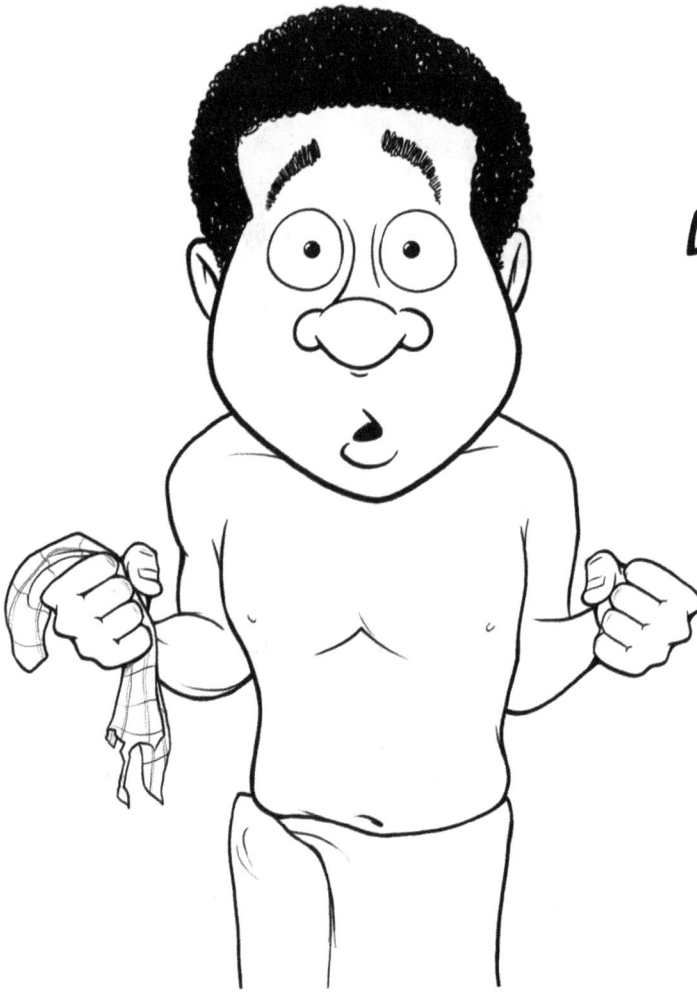

DADDY

"Daddy!"

So I wrapped myself in my towel,
and I went to greet her kindly.

"I just want you to know," she said,
as I stood there cold and soggy.

"I love you up to heaven
'cause you let us have a doggie."

Nina, Nina, you've never seen a dog like Nina. What a pet.

If I won't play, she looks for a way
to make me very upset.

But I guess we'll keep her yet
'cause my kids sure love their pet.

And to tell you the truth,
I also love my pet!

Has anyone seen my wallet?
Yup, that's my dog Nina!

Wasn't There a Dog in the Bible?

Wasn't there a dog in the Bible
with Adam and Eve with the snake?
Ssss, Ssss, Ssss.

Making all the noise he could make.
Raur, raur, raur.

Trying to stop their big mistake.

Woof, woof, woof!
Woof, woof, woof!

And wasn't there a dog in the Bible
when Noah built the Ark?
Konk, konk, konk.

And the sky was getting dark?
Boom, boom, boom.

Rounding up the animals
with a bark.
Raur, raur, raur!
Raur, raur, raur!

Wasn't there a dog in the Bible
on Christmas night with the sheep?

Baa, Baa, Baa.

When the shepherds fell asleep.

Zzzzz, Zzzzzzz!

Till the angels came and
made them leap.
Ahh! Ahh!

Wasn't there a dog in the Bible
that helped them find their way?
Raur, raur, raur!

To the place where Jesus lay.

Shhhhh! It's a baby!

Bringing us a brighter day.
Yay, Yay!

I wouldn't be surprised if you read between the lines.

The must have been a dog
right there every time!

What do you think?
Well, you never know!

Jonah and the Whale!

Jonah was a prophet from the ancient land of Israel.
"Jonah," said the Lord, "Go preach against the city of Nineveh.
It has become very wicked."

"No way!" said Jonah. He turned
around and ran from the Lord.

He found a ship headed far away.
He paid his fare, and then he
climbed aboard.

But the Lord sent a powerful
wind to break up the ship.

When the sailors discovered that
Jonah was running away from
the Lord, they threw him overboard!

SPLASH!

Down, down, deep into the sea
he went. The Lord sent a huge whale
to swallow Jonah . . . GULP!

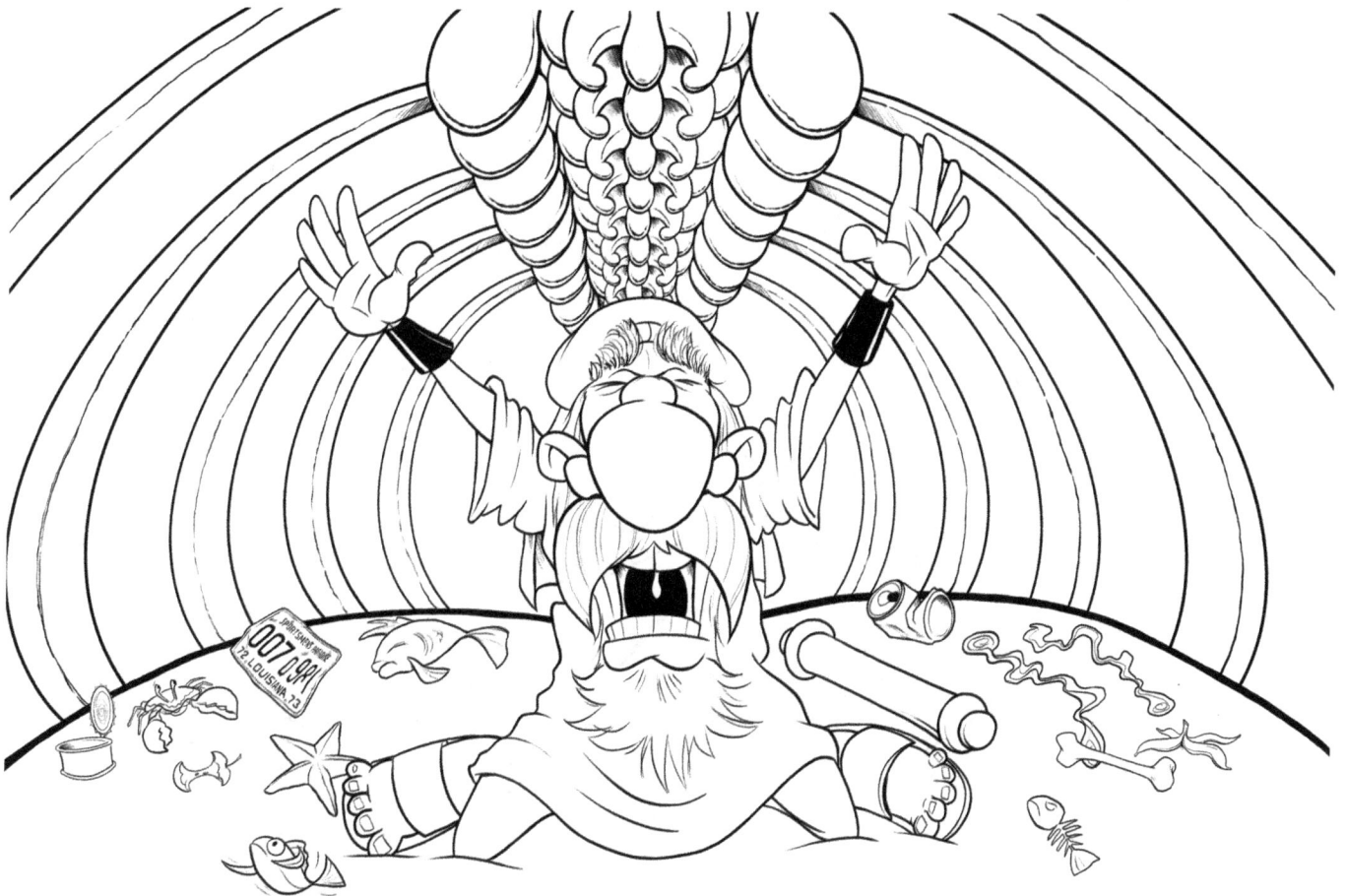

"When my life was ebbing away,
I called out to the Lord.
I promised to obey and preach
to the city of Nineveh."

Then the Lord commanded the
whale, and it vomited Jonah
onto dry land!

So Jonah went immediately to
Nineveh, and he started to preach.
"Repent and obey God, or God
will punish you!" said Jonah.

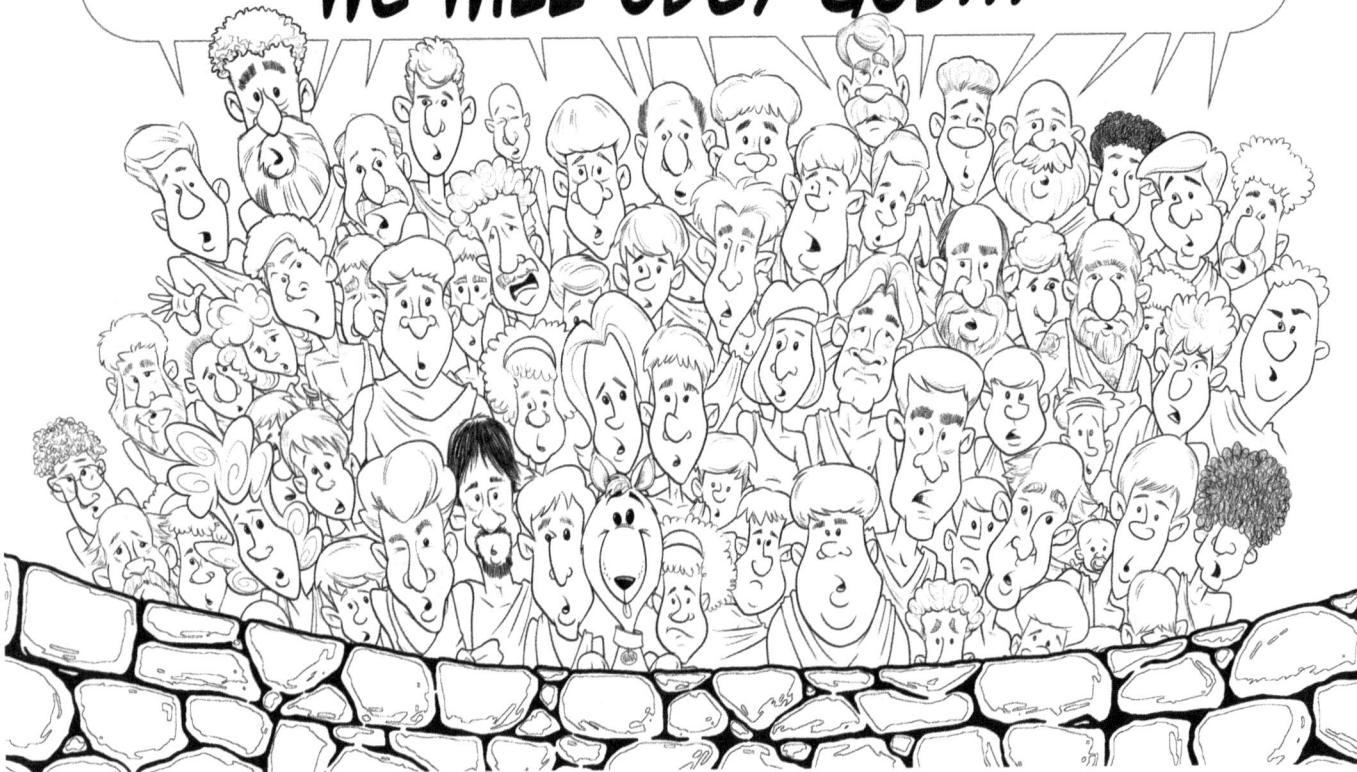

"We will! We will obey God,"
said the people of Nineveh.

When God saw that the people had turned away from their wickedness, God relented and did not destroy them.

And so, here's the lesson:
If you hear the voice of God,
be sure to obey. Don't be like
Jonah who ended up in the
belly of a whale!

What is Liberty?

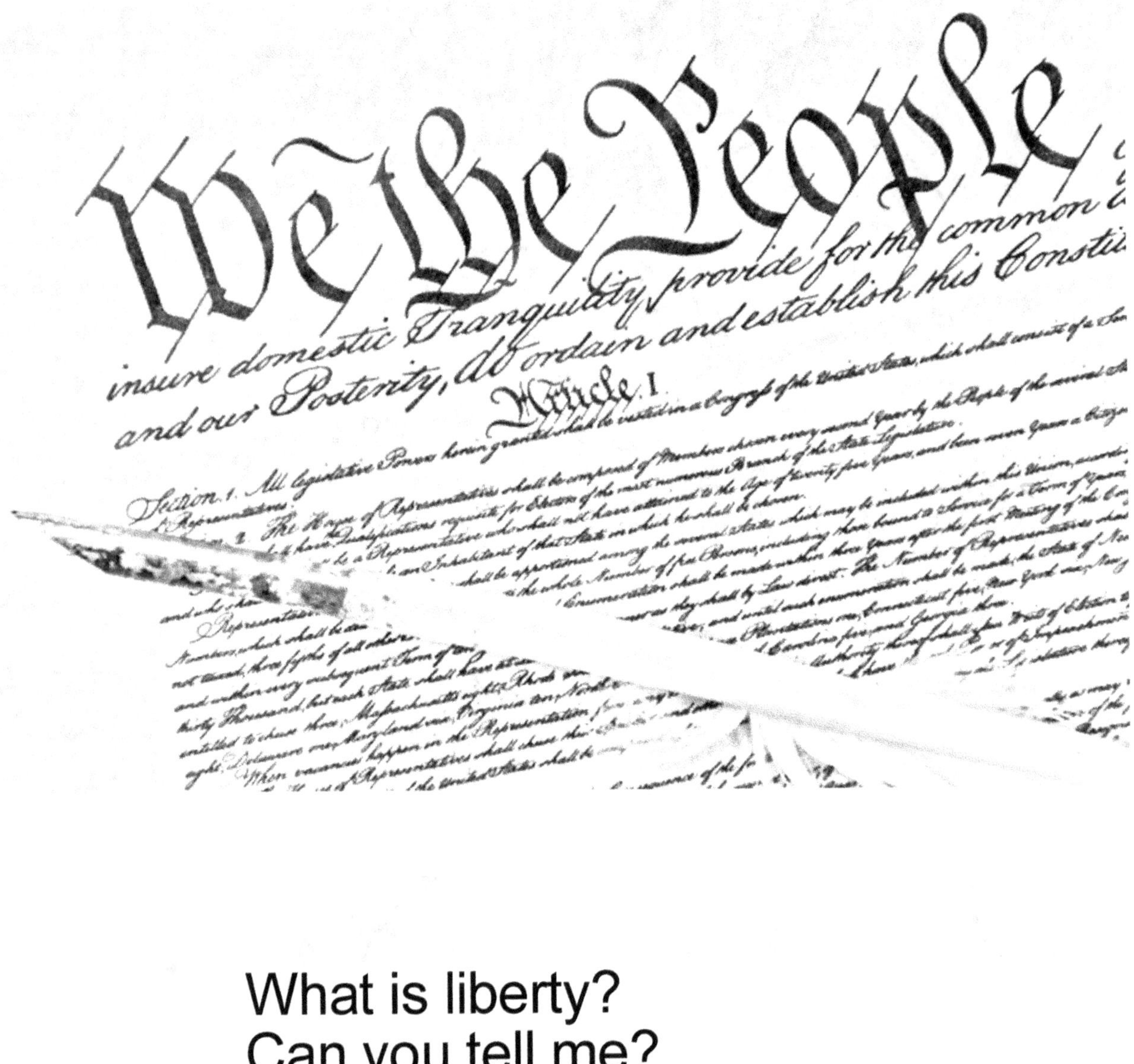

What is liberty?
Can you tell me?
What makes us free?

Is it something government gives us?
Or a right given by God to me?

Come with me, sing a song with me.
We want you to come along,
and answer the question,
"What is liberty?"

What is history?
Can you tell me?
What makes a nation?

Is it only heroes and villains, children?
Or also God's creation?

Come with me.
Sing a song with me.
We want you to come along,
and answer the question,
"What is history?"

And answer the question,
"What is liberty?"

OFFICER DO-GOOD

www.ingramcontent.com/pod-product-compliance
Lightning Source LLC
Chambersburg PA
CBHW080524030426
42337CB00023B/4619